The Identity of a CHRISTIAN

Terrell Taylor

THE IDENTITY OF A CHRISTIAN

© 2022 by Terrell Taylor

Printed in the United States of America

All right reserved. No part of this publication may be reproduced, stored in a retrieval system, or transmitted in any form or by any means-electronic, digital, photocopy, recording, or any other- except for brief quotations in printed reviews, without the prior written permission of the author.

All Scripture quotations, unless otherwise stated, are taken from the King James Version. Copyright © 1982 by Thomas Nelson, Inc. Used by permission. All rights reserved.

Front & Back Cover Art & Book Interior Designed by Krystle Laughter, LLC
krystlelaughter.org

ISBN
978-1-955787-12-3

The purpose of this book:

The purpose of this book is to reveal the identity and irresistible power that Christians are given the moment they receive Jesus Christ. You will find no chapters in this book, only one unified text of truth and power. That way, what you read is fully perceived and not broken up, giving you a clear picture of who God says you are.

This book is short but powerful and can be easily read daily to remind yourself of who you are after reading God's word.

A Special Thanks

Thank you so much to the people who allowed me to share their testimonies to build the faith of those reading this book. I love you so much.

Table of Contents

Introduction..7

Opening Prayer..9

Testimonials..13-19

Identity..21

Christ..29

God..33

Victorious...41

Authority..47

Closing Prayer..55

About the Author...59

Become an Author..63

Introduction

Kings and Queens, I pray your faith is stirred and strengthened because this is the life that God intended for us to have. I live this life progressively, invincibly, and victoriously every day because I know who Jesus says we are, and I believe it. By the end of this book, you will too.

What I'm about to tell you is extremely simple. If you catch it in its simplicity, it will unlock the incredible, unbreakable, and invincible power that Jesus placed in you the day you believed in Him. It is written, "And what is the EXCEEDING GREATNESS of HIS POWER in us who believe, according to the working of his MIGHTY POWER" (Ephesians 1:19).

God is extremely mighty and unlimitedly POWERFUL. He has placed in each of us who believe His EXCEEDINGLY GREAT AND MIGHTY POWER. This plays a huge part in who we are.

Opening Prayer

Father, in the mighty name of Jesus Christ, thank you for loving me and making me to live for your glory. I love you.

By the authority of Jesus Christ, whatever demonic spirit and satanic powers are limiting and blocking my mind and heart from receiving and believing God's word be BROKEN and DESTROYED by the blood of Jesus.

I command my heart and mind to be open and receive the Holy Spirit and what your word is saying in Jesus' mighty name. Father, let me see who you say I am according to your word, and help me to be a doer of your word. In Jesus' mighty name. Amen!

Let me first say that I am extremely excited for you. I'm incredibly excited for you to discover who God intentionally created you to be. It's very important for you to understand what it means to be a Christian. Christians LIVE Jesus. As it is written, "to LIVE is Christ..." (Philippians 1:21) and again, "Christ is our LIFE..." (Colossians 3:4). As a Christian, Christ is who we follow and live, not just who we believe. This is a very important truth.

Christians don't profess Jesus then LIVE contrary to his word. This doesn't mean that we don't sin. It simply means that no matter what, we get up from our fallen state (repent) and continue with living Jesus. As it is written, "For a RIGHTEOUS man FALLS seven times, but rises up again..." (Proverbs 24:16).

God still classifies a man as RIGHTEOUS even though he sinned, if he gets up and continues walking in righteousness. Now that we've covered that, let's uncover who we are. Nothing in the world is more exciting, certain, or powerful than becoming a Christian. I'll tell you why in a moment.

First, I will say that one of the most destructive things that can happen in your life as a Christian is not knowing your identity. By not knowing who God says you are, you will base your identity on what you feel, think, or the opinions of others. Even worse on the destructive things, the devil attempts to do to your life. You may even go so far as measuring your life by the possessions and materials things you have which come and go.

This is a confusing, unstable, and self-destructive way to live. It's like changing who you are every time the wind changes direction; a powerless and defeated life. I'm not speaking from what I've heard or seen. I'm speaking from what I've experienced and how I live.

By simply believing who God says I am, I can change the direction and outcome of any opposition that arises in my life. Through this same belief, I can also impact the lives of others I'm sent to. I can demonstrate signs, wonders, and miracles by standing on God's word. I've demonstrated the power of the Holy Spirit by casting out demons and healing the sick with a word. My wife and I even raised a dead person to life by simply commanding. All this is possible by just believing in who God says we are.

To stir your faith even more, I've included some brief testimonials from others. These are stories of what God has allowed me to do by his power and by simply knowing and believing who he says we are.

Testimonials

Donna's Testimony

Hi, my name is Donna. I am Terrell's mom. This story is one of the many instances that I was delivered through my son praying for me. I had a car parked outside my friend's house that wouldn't start for several years. One day a tow truck was sent to tow it away. I happened to be walking to my friend's house at that time. As I saw what was happening, I ran and asked the driver to give me some time to move the car. He said, "I will be back tomorrow. If it's not gone, I will tow it."

    I called my son, Terrell, to help me move it. After we talked for a little while, he told me there was a demon on the car, which is why it wouldn't start. He said to call him back when it started. He hung up and began to pray. He cursed the demon and commanded it out of the car. He told the car to start.

I waited a little bit and then tried to start the car. The car started for the first time in years. I was in complete shock! Then the car began to sputter and shut off. When I called him to tell him what was happening, he said, "Praise God. When it starts, call me."

He hung up and prayed again. Just like that, it started up. I called him singing and laughing with so much joy. I could barely believe it. That day I saw God's power could do anything. I thank Jesus for the miracle. I thank God for my son.

Joseph & Lissa's Testimony

My name is Joseph, and my wife's name is Lissa. We went to doctors and were told that my wife had cancer in her lymphoid and bones. It was devastating news! We did not claim anything the doctor was saying. We know the devil is a liar.

Praise God for my brother Anthony Wright. He asked if he could introduce me to a strong man of God and a prayer warrior named Terrell. We agreed. From that point on, it was truly a blessing. Terrell prayed with us multiple times. First with me and then with my wife. Before he prayed, he told me that my wife would be healed. He also said that if anything contrary to the word of God enters our life, it is from satan.

He said satan is the cause of all sickness and disease and that we have authority over all of his power. Satan must obey our command.

I was driving when Terrell asked if he could pray. I said yes and pulled into a parking lot. He started praying, and as he was praying, I felt the Holy Spirit's anointing. It was so powerful that I wanted to jump out of the car and run around the parking lot. I felt the Spirit of the Lord, and it was an incredible feeling!

Terrell asked if I could call later so he could pray with my wife, and I said yes. I called later, and he started praying for my wife. He cursed cancer and commanded it to come out. He commanded the spirit of infirmity and disease to be bound and broken. He said, "By the stripes of Jesus, you are healed." He commanded everything to be recreated.

My wife said she was feeling hot, and I told her, "It's God healing you." I am proud to say, through prayer and supplication, her test results for cancer came back NEGATIVE!

I praise God's holy name! Thank you, Jesus, for putting Terrell in our lives, and thank you, Jesus, for everyone else who was praying for us. I have pictures of the paperwork that shows cancer and the paperwork that shows NO cancer. HALLELUJAH!

CANCER

KAISER PERMANENTE

Date printed: 11/15/2021
Kaiser Permanente
Member name: M Lissa Wright
Date of birth: 12/17/1968
MRN:

For general information about a test procedure, click the "About this test" link above.

To see more information about a test result, select the "Details" tab. To compare test results over time, click "Past results" or "Graph of past results."

Minor differences in test results from the usual range are not uncommon and likely represent acceptable individual or lab variation. Test results outside the usual range are subject to interpretation by your doctor.

1. There are findings suspicious for metastatic involvement of the mediastinal lymph nodes, lungs, and bones.
2. Mildly to moderately hypermetabolic mediastinal and bilateral hilar lymph nodes are suspicious for metastatic involvement.
3. Multiple minimally to mildly hypermetabolic nodules in the lungs bilaterally, right greater than left, are suspicious for metastatic involvement.
4. Multiple moderately to intensely hypermetabolic osseous lesions in the axial skeleton with no clear associated CT abnormalities are suspicious for metastatic osseous involvement.

NO CANCER

KAISER PERMANENTE

kp.org/messagecenter

To Bronchoscopy Results
CHARLES POON MD
M Lissa Wright
09/29/2021

Hi Lissa. I could not reach you today to discuss your bronchoscopy results. The findings show granulomatous inflammation which is considered a benign finding. There was no evidence of cancer. Results will be forwarded to your physicians at Redwood City for review. Let me know if you have any questions about these results or prefer to discuss anything by phone.

Thanks.
Charles

Donicha's Testimony

My name is Donicha, Terrell's younger sister. I contracted a stomach infection that was causing me anxiety. Because of past pains from my youth, I drank myself into a declining state of health. The more I tried to climb out of the hole of addiction, the deeper the addiction pulled me down into darkness and despair.

I remember laying in the hospital bed with my phone glued to my ear as my brother prayed and prophesied over me. Little by little, I saw my life restored. Healing entered my body. Where there used to be burning and pain, my stomach was now healed.

As long as I live, I will be eternally thankful! I am grateful that God allowed me to be born into the same family as Terrell Taylor, a mighty man of valor and unshakeable faith.

Identity

Identity

Understand that God's desire and intention for you was established from the very beginning. He intentionally created you "in his own image and AFTER his likeness" (Genesis 1:26). With this, He also "gave you dominion over all of the Earth" (Genesis 1:26).

    To have dominion means to rule, master, govern, and control. To be in the image of God is to look like him and to reflect him. To be AFTER his likeness is to be LIKE him. It is an honor and great privilege to reflect and be made AFTER the ALMIGHTY GOD. This alone should flood your heart with overwhelming joy! God's own words show us his intention for us from the very start was for us to be like him.

This view and understanding are seen throughout scripture. For instance, it is written that "Christ is the head and we are his body the church" (Colossians 1:18). The head and the body are ONE. It is written, "For as the body is ONE and has many members, and all the members of that one body, being many, are ONE body: so also is Christ" (1 Corinthians 12:27). Because all of the parts of the body are ONE, they share ONE identity.

The identity of the head is the identity of the body, and this head happens to be Christ. This means that his body (us) is who Christ is. That's why it is written, "...as Christ IS so are we in this world" (1 John 4:17). It makes perfect sense that we are exactly as he is because we are HIS body. Doesn't your body share your identity? Aren't your head and your body identified as one? So, it makes sense that who Christ is, we are also, since we are his body. Don't forget the end of this scripture, which drives it home. It reads "in this world," implying that in this reality: we are as Christ is.

Another passage in scripture states, "We are individual parts of HIS body, of HIS flesh and of HIS bones" (Ephesians 5:30). Think about it, being the flesh and bones of someone makes you that person. For example, if you were a lion's flesh and bones, wouldn't that make you that lion? Say you were the flesh and bones of a thief; wouldn't that make you that thief?

But it explicitly says, "we are members of HIS body, of HIS flesh, and of HIS bones" (Ephesians 5:30). It means we are him!

This is why it is also written, "He who has been baptized INTO Christ has PUT ON Christ" (Galatians 3:27). If you put on Christ, don't you become him? And again, "Don't you know that your bodies are the members of Christ's body? Shall I then take the body parts of Christ and join them to a prostitute? God forbid" (1 Corinthians 6:15-17). This scripture refers to you as his body parts, and what you do as his body parts, you do to him.

I hope it is clear by now that being Christ's body makes you him. God even refers to Christ as his arm "Behold, the Lord God comes with might, and HIS ARM (Christ) rules for him." If we have become Christ by being his flesh and bones (his body), then how true is the scripture that says, "It's no longer I that lives, but Christ" (Galatians 12:20). This is AMAZING!!!

There is another meaning. God is not only saying we are who Jesus is, but also his character is our character. We are holy as he is holy; righteous as he is righteous; and perfect as he is perfect.

Who we were, with all of our mistakes, shame, guilt, and sins, are no more because we are now him because we are his body.

That is why it is written, "If any man be IN Christ, he is a new creature. The old is gone, and the new has come" (2 Corinthians 5:17). Your body is his body, so you no longer exist. WHAT A GIFT FROM JESUS!!! By default, we inherit his character, personality, and power. We inherit the literal FULLNESS of him simply by being the body of him. HALLELUJAH!

The Bible says, "of his FULLNESS have we all received" (John 1:16). Why? Because we've become him. All of these scriptures align and confirm that who we are as Christians is fully Christ in the flesh with all his power. There is so much more to us than just believing in Christ and going to heaven.

If it's not clear to you by now, this also means you share in the GOD-HEAD because you are Christ's body. It is written in scripture "For in him (Christ) dwells all the fullness of the Godhead bodily" (Colossians 2:9). If this is who he is, and you are the body of him (his flesh and bone), then this is who you are too.

Jesus himself said, "And the GLORY which you gave me I have GIVEN THEM; that they may be one, even as we are one: I in them, and you in me" (John 17:22-23). The same glory that the Father gave Jesus, Jesus gave to us. Why? Because we are his body. We are one with him.

Because we are one with Him, we share His identity, His glory, and His power. There is unthinkable and immeasurable power dwelling in you. With this power, you can create, overthrow, shift or tear down anything you will if you command it to be so.

Simply put, what doesn't obey God when he speaks to it? If we are ONE with him, what wouldn't obey our command? There is absolutely no limit to the possibilities and power that dwells in you as it is written, "...NOTHING shall be impossible unto you" (Matthew 17:20).

Let me make this very clear. Apart from Christ and outside of him, we are NOTHING. Because he MADE us to be LIKE him and IN him just as it is written, "For in him we live, and move, and have our BEING" (Acts 17:58). This may shock many of you, but it is the truth.

We are commanded to live by nothing else but God's word as it's written: "...we live not by bread alone but by every word that comes out of the mouth of God" (Deuteronomy 8:3) and "let God be true and every man a liar" (Romans 3:4). Understand as God has written it, this is who we are.

Now that the foundation of Christ has been laid, the next part will take you deeper. You now know that you are the body of Jesus which makes you him. Let's find out who he is!

Let me say this; you can't know who you are without knowing who he is. Knowing who he is, is knowing who you are because you're his body. His identity is your identity.

Christ

Christ

So who is Christ? Christ says, "ALL power and authority in heaven and earth has been given to me" (Matthew 28:18). This means that all of the power and authority that exists in heaven and earth has been given to Christ. This alone makes him SUPREME and ALL powerful.

So what does this mean for you? If you're the body of Christ, which makes you him, then this is who you are as well! You have been given the same SUPREME power and authority by simply being the body of Christ. Is it not written that "God raised us up with Christ and seated us with him in the heavenly realms IN Christ Jesus?" (Ephesians 2:6-7). We sit in the same seat he sits in.

Think about it. Where you are sitting, your body parts sit with you. To prove we share in his power, look at what comes with the seat we sit in with Christ.

"God raised Christ from the dead, and SAT him at his own right hand in the heavenly places, FAR ABOVE ALL principality and power, and might, and dominion, and every name that is named, not only in this world but also in that which is to come" (Ephesians 1:21). Can you see how mighty and powerful God intentionally made you in Christ?

There is NOTHING more powerful or stronger than us in Christ. Christ has POWER over ALL things, and we being his body and seated with him, do too. If you know this and believe it, the pains and problems of your life will have no choice but to bow to you and submit to your command!

Now let's go even deeper. It is written, "He who is joined to the Lord (God) has become ONE spirit with him" (1 Corinthians 6:17). If you're one with Jesus, you've become one spirit with God. Remember, "God is spirit" (John 4:24). If you think of who God is and the power he contains, your top should blow because it says specifically, you become ONE SPIRIT WITH HIM. This is further confirmation that you share in the Godhead.

God

God

Let's look at what it says God is. It is written, "...upon the likeness of the throne was the likeness as the appearance of a man above upon it. The appearance of fire round about within it, his body I saw as it were the appearance of fire, and it had brightness round about" (Ezekiel 1:14), "And out of the throne proceeded lightning and thundering..." (Revelation 4:5). Look at what we've become ONE with! How can we not be INCREDIBLY POWERFUL?

    To become ONE with God is to become SUPREME in power. Jesus says, "I am in the Father, and the Father is in me" (John 14:11). If we are in Christ and Christ is in the Father, and the Father is in Christ, are we not all ONE?

One day Phillip asked Jesus, "Show us the Father, and it will be enough." Jesus said to him, "have I been so long with you, Phillip, and you have not recognized me, he who has seen me has seen the Father" (John 14:8). What Jesus is saying is that precisely who God is and is like, he is and is like because he and the Father are ONE.

Jesus also said, "Believe me when I say I am in the father and the father is in me or at least believe in the evidence of the miracles themselves..." (John 14:11). Jesus was saying that the power and miracles he displayed proved that he is one with the father. This means that if we are one with the Father in Christ, this is also the power we contain and the abilities we have.

As it is written, "He who believes in me, the things I do he will do and greater things will he do, for I go to the Father" (John 14:12). Again, it is written, "..as many as received him, to them gave he POWER to become the sons of God" (John 1:12). It is evident that we share in God's supreme and unlimited power. You should be OVERJOYED because God is telling you that he desires you to be like him.

Tell me, how is it possible for us to be weak, broken, and defeated having all of this POWER? Is Jesus or God weak, broken, and defeated? NO!!! So then, how can we be if we are one with him? This is why it's written, "You are more than conquerors through him" (Romans 8:37).

What can conquer him? You are in him, so all that he is and can do, you are and can do. It is even written "... Christ is the firstborn of many brothers and sisters" (Romans 8:29). Meaning He is the FIRST born of many that are like him. You are created, chosen, and GREATLY privileged to be the spitting image of Christ himself on this earth.

This is why it is also written: "...we are being conformed into the image of Christ" (Romans 8:29). This is very POWERFUL.

You should be ready to pull down strongholds, break limitations and barriers, and command things to manifest. Let's keep going. It also states, "You are dead, and your life is hidden with Christ inside God" (Colossians 13:3). This makes you one with God. Being dead means not to exist, and being hidden means not being seen. God is saying that who you were is dead and who you are now is inside of him with Christ. AMAZING!! This means there is no more you, only God.

It's time to recognize that everything about you is God. It is an INCREDIBLE honor to become ONE with God ALMIGHTY in Christ! It is clear why this scripture is written, "I have said, Ye are gods; and all of you are children of the most High..." (Psalm 82:6).

Extreme glory and power dwells in Christians from our ONENESS with God in Christ. How foolishly low do we think of ourselves compared to what God thinks of us? With this understanding, it's impossible for you to ever think mediocre of yourself again. Thinking low of yourself is thinking low of God because you are ONE with him. It's also written, "we are the light of the WORLD and a city on a hilltop that can't be hidden" (Matthew 5:14).

"God is light, and in him there is no darkness at all" (1 John 1:5). So, of course, you are the light of the world if you are ONE with him who is light itself. Furthermore, how can we who are ONE with him and share in so much power and glory not shine?

What else does the Bible say about Christ? It's written, "Christ is the image of the invisible God, the firstborn of every creature: For by him were ALL THINGS CREATED, that are in heaven, and that are in earth, visible and invisible, whether they be thrones, or dominions, or principalities, or powers: ALL things were CREATED BY HIM, and for him: And he is before all things, and BY HIM all things consist" (Colossians 1:15-17).

Now, I am in no way stating that we've created all things. This is to outline and show the immense, unspeakable, and irresistible power that we share in and are connected to by being the body of Christ. It also states, "...Christ is the head of EVERY power and authority" (Colossians 2:10). So not only has every power and authority in heaven and earth been GIVEN to him, but he's also the HEAD of all power and authority.

We now know what a MIGHTY MIGHTY MIGHTY God that we are ONE with. What could we possibly fear that is under our power?

Jesus has the power to enforce obedience in all of creation. It is written, "God has put ALL things under his feet and gave him to be the HEAD over ALL things to the church" (Ephesians 1:22). Christ is the head of ALL THINGS, and all things are under his command.

By now, as the identity of Christ is being disclosed to you, it should be clear to see who you truly are. This is who we are and who God called us to be. The anointing is so heavy right now. WOOOO JESUUUUSSSS, HALLELUJAAAAHHHH. I have to stop and give Him praise and glory.

Every time I remind myself of who I am in him, a jolt of refreshing electricity shoots to my heart and runs through my whole body. It leaves a joyful, loving feeling that renews my mind in power. It is difficult to explain, but it's powerful and feels good. Thank you, daddy! (God). I love you so much!

Victorious

Victorious

Now you can see who God intentionally made you to be and what you possess because of oneness with Christ. What "weapon would you concern yourself with, that would ever be able to prosper against you?" (Isaiah 54:17). Why would sickness, disease, poverty, death, or anything else concern you? Don't make me laugh.

Are we not the head of all these things by being one in Christ? What is our concern? What in existence could stand against you and win? The very thought of ever being defeated by anything with our identity in Christ is laughable! There is no opposition in existence that would not give way to your command being one with Christ the HEAD and SUPREME of ALL things.

God wants you to see how extremely powerful and wonderful he intentionally made you to be! With this truth, we have truly become INVINCIBLE.

Now that you know you are ONE with God, it's very important that you think like him. This is the key to being able to walk in your identity. It is even written, "...Be transformed by the renewing of your mind" (Romans 12:2). What you renew your mind with, you transform into. If you renew your mind with sickness, you become sick. If you renew your mind with poverty, you become poor. If you renew your mind with anger and defeat, you become angry and defeated. Whatever you renew your mind with, you transform into.

Renew your mind with your new identity in Christ. If we are his body, then we should always have his thinking. As it's written, "we have the mind of Christ" (1 Corinthians 2:16). We should never entertain thoughts that are not his. Our lives depend on it.

As I said at the beginning of this book, "I live invincibly and victoriously". Know that every word that I spoke is true. How can I not be invincible, knowing who I truly am in Christ? It doesn't matter what arises in my life, I have absolute power over it because I am ONE with Christ.

Although sometimes your opposition is permitted by God to linger a little while so that your faith is built up and strengthened in him, as it is written, "Let patience have her perfect work that you may be PERFECT and COMPLETE not lacking anything" (James 1:3-4).

It's purposed for us to go through the situation, not to destroy us, but to strengthen our faith and refine our character. In no way are you to let up in exercising your authority over your opposition. Stand in your power and continue to command that opposition to give way, and it will in Jesus Mighty Name.

To prove this, let me paraphrase a time in Christ's life when he demonstrated having authority over his storm (trials and tribulations) in a boat with his disciples. I'll first tell you why I believe his storm represented trials and tribulations. The same analogy is used in another passage that talks about the security of one's home who builds on the rock and the other on the sand. The waves and the winds beat against both houses alike, but the one who built on the rock withstood his storm, and the other crashed GREATLY.

The believer and non-believer alike face the same trials and tests of life. The only difference is the one who built his house on the rock withstood his trials and overcame them. Storms represent the trials and tribulations of life. This is why I call Christ's storm "trials and tribulations".

Back to the story about Jesus on a boat with his disciples. The storm was so crazy that the disciples thought they would die with God (Christ), the HEAD of ALL things, right there in the boat with them. That's how crazy this storm was.

Jesus stood to his feet, stretched out his hand, and SPOKE to his storm (trials and tribulations) "Peace, be still." His storm instantly died, and there was a GREAT CALM. Instantly the waves dropped and became still, the clouds vanished, the winds died, and the sun instantly shone brightly. ABSOLUTELY INCREDIBLE.

He did all this by being one with God; because he is one with God, he simply spoke and changed the outcome of his storm. It's even written in another passage where Jesus was in another storm, but this time, he walked on the waves and told Peter to come out on the water with him (Matthew 14:24-29). Here he demonstrated that we have ABSOLUTE power over our storms and further confirmed it when he told Peter to walk on top of the waves with him.

Remember, "he who believes in me, the things that I do he will do and GREATER things will he do..." (John 14:12). We not only have the power to easily command our storm to change and have it obey us, but we are never to be overcome by them.

Authority

Authority

God has revealed to you your true identity, but this next part is equally important. It could even be the difference between life and death if you don't know it. There is a way that a Christian, being one with Christ and having all this power, can live a life of disease, poverty, and defeat. Let me say first, satan is the cause of everything destructive, evil, and contrary to God's word that comes into your life, such as sickness, disease, death, poverty, pain, fear, anxiety, depression, limitation, doubt, and unbelief.

    It was necessary for me to give you a small list so you can have a clearer understanding of the things that satan is behind in people's lives. It is written, "satan comes to do nothing but steal, kill and destroy" (John 10:10). If anything in your life fits these categories, satan is there.

Let me tell you what a fantastic thing it is that satan comes to do this. It is written, "Behold I give you authority to tread on snakes and scorpions (demonic spirits) and OVER ALL of the power of the devil and NOTHING by any means shall hurt you at all" (Luke10:19). Everything that is within satan's power we have AUTHORITY OVER. This means the authority to bind, break and destroy anything he's doing in our lives. We can restore what he destroyed with a command.

God allows him to come our way because he's the instrument God uses to exercise our power and authority. Authority means "to enforce obedience", so basically, we have the power to enforce satan and all his kingdom to obey our command. This is total victory over the kingdom of darkness! What can satan do to us that we don't have power over to reverse? He's under OUR authority!

If we've been given authority over ALL of his power, how can he ever have power over us? Hmm! It's simply not possible. But as I said, there is a way for a Christian with this INCREDIBLE POWER to live a life of disease, poverty, and defeat. I'll get to that shortly. I will further say, if God said he gave YOU the authority over the devil and all his power, then understand that what the devil is allowed to do in your life is up to you.

God indeed has the authority to deliver you, but if he gave YOU the authority, it's now on you.

For example, Moses was at the red sea and told the Israelites, "the Egyptians that you see today you will see no more. Be still and see the salvation of the Lord". He was very confident that God was about to deliver them. Moses turned to God, and God said something incredible back to him. God said, "why are you crying to me? Stretch the staff I GAVE YOU, divide the sea and go on dry ground".

I can imagine the face of Moses as if to say, "What do you mean, why am I crying to you? Clearly, you're our deliverer God". This was a very powerful thing for God to say since Moses was looking to God to deliver them. God was waiting on Moses to do it.

In other words, Moses' victory or defeat was in his own hands after God handed over the staff (authority) to him. It's that way for us. God has placed satan under your authority. It's up to you to command him out of your life. If you don't give him a command, he will never move! He will stay in your life and steal, kill and destroy you until you pass away.

Now, you may be thinking, "What if he doesn't go when I command him to?" What I will say to you is that it's very possible that he will try to resist you. He will make it appear he's not going anywhere, nor is he going to stop anything he's doing in your life. I tell you the truth; it's a BLUFF. He cannot go beyond the word of God. The truth remains, "you have authority OVER ALL his power" (John 10:10).

Understand this will NEVER change no matter what satan is appearing to do. He must obey your command! You stand on God's word and keep commanding him as one who has authority over him. He will break and flee from you as it is written "Submit to God (believe him and his word). RESIST the devil, and he will flee" (James 4:7).

Furthermore, God can't lie, so everything that opposes his word is a BLUFF. It is also written, "Let God be true and every man a liar" (Rom 3:4). When God says something, the opposition has no choice but to bow. Just like God told Moses, Pharaoh would let them go, but at the same time, Pharaoh was saying no. Like clockwork, at God's time, Pharaoh let them go. When He says something, consider it ALREADY done.

How about when God's word prevailed against the limitations of Abraham's body at 100 years old and caused him to have a son? Regardless of the limitations of Abraham's body and age of 100 years old, God's word prevailed, and Abraham had a son. Regardless of the opposition in your life or satan's resisting you, stand on God's word, and you will never be defeated.

Satan only prevails in your life if you move off of the word of God and give in to his BLUFF. Now, I told you two times before that there is a way for a Christian with this incredible power in them to live a life of disease, poverty, and defeat.

Here it is. "We are destroyed for our lack of knowledge" (Hosea 4:6). Our lack of knowing who God says we are can destroy us.

Satan has not only convinced the church that we have no authority over the destruction he brings to our lives (so we say it's God's will), but he has convinced some of us that he's a fairy tale that doesn't exist at all. Recognize the danger in this. If I believe this garbage, I will never recognize when satan is wreaking havoc in my life. I'll chalk up every evil thing that occurs in my life as God's will. And if it's God's will, how can I trust him or believe he's for my good?

Get this, even prayer will go out the window if I believe satan doesn't exist or it's THE WILL of God and what is supposed to be will be. That is ABSOLUTELY ABSURD! If it is written that God gave me authority over satan, doesn't that clarify that he's real and that I have power over him?

This poisonous deception is the perfect storm for satan to live in your life and destroy it. That's why God says, "be SOBER be WATCHFUL for your adversary the devil is roaming about like a roaring lion seeking for someone to devour" (1 Peter 5:8). If you don't believe that satan is real or that you have power over him, you're his favorite food.

Satan will feed sweetly on you, and you will live a life of total defeat, hopelessness, depression, sickness, disease, and poverty until the day you go to heaven.

You can indeed believe in Jesus and go to heaven, but you will live like hell here on earth until you get there and will never fulfill the purpose and destiny God designed for you. Let me tell you what frustrates God. Since he has made himself ONE with you, God is forced to surrender and bow with you when you choose to bow to the devil in defeat.

Remember, "He will never leave you nor forsake you" (Hebrews 13:5). When you bow, God bows. This alone disarms the power of God in your life. It's even written "..to who you yield yourselves servants to obey, his servant you are to who you obey" (Romans 6:16). If you surrender to satan he is your master, and God's power is surrendered with you. As you can see how frustrated God could be and why satan hopes you never see him.

Satan's greatest power on earth is in what you don't know (your ignorance). Ignorance is not bliss. It is destruction. Not knowing who God says we are or not knowing his word destroys us. PERIOD.

As I told you at the beginning of this book, "There is nothing in the world more exciting, more certain, or more powerful than becoming a Christian." And other than Jesus, nothing has been more true. BE CHANGED FOREVER IN JESUS JESUS MIGHTY NAME!

Closing Prayer

Prayer

Jesus, thank you that you love me so much. Thank you for your word and your truth. Father, I receive it right now in the mighty name of Jesus Christ.

I repent and ask for forgiveness for any sins I have committed against you. Cleanse me of all unrighteousness. Thank you, Father.

I speak to the old man and the old way of thinking, DIE and be uprooted and removed from me now in the mighty name of Jesus Christ! I renounce the lies of satan, and I break any covenant or agreement I had with him. In the mighty name of Jesus Christ, his connection to my life in any way be destroyed.

By the blood of Jesus, I receive the real me. I command the light of God and who he says I am to come alive in me now in the mighty name of Jesus Christ.

I am as you are, Jesus. As you are holy, righteous, powerful, anointed, wealthy, favored, and blessed, so am I.

I receive who you say I am now in the mighty name of Jesus Christ. Thank you, Lord. In Jesus' name, Amen.

ABOUT THE AUTHOR

Terrell Taylor is a husband, father, author, and compassionate powerful man of God. He is well known in his community for his heart for Jesus and his love for people. Through his ministry, Created To Reign, he ministers the word of God and heals the sick through the power of the Holy Spirit. Terrell Taylor was born in Kansas City, Missouri, and raised in Seattle, WA; He was saved at the tender age of nine and has followed Jesus wholeheartedly since then.

Terrell is also a gospel music artist (JusPraise) and released his album titled: Amazing Love. He was nominated for Best Artist at the ITM Awards. He resides in Washington with his beautiful wife Lanaya and their three amazing children. You can check him out on his social media @TerrellTaylor on Facebook and @agloriousking on TikTok.

AMAZING LOVE

INCLUDING THE HIT SINGLE "LORD, YOUR MY FRIEND"

AVAILABLE ON ALL STREAMING PLATFORMS!

Become an Author

Do you want to write a book, help others, and create extra income? Hi, my name is Krystle Laughter, and I make it easy for ordinary people to become authors. Writing and self-publishing a book doesn't have to be complicated. Let me walk you through the step-by-step process from start to finish. You can work with me one-on-one or through my online courses at Krystle Laughter Academy.

Becoming an author changed my life, and it can change yours too. Through writing my story, I've been able to help over 5,000+ people heal. Additionally, my books bring in thousands of dollars each month in passive income. With God, nothing is impossible. If you're serious about self-publishing your book and becoming an author, Join the academy today!

Krystle Laughter Academy

Become an Author, create extra Income & make an IMPACT!

KRYSTLELAUGHTER.ORG

www.ingramcontent.com/pod-product-compliance
Lightning Source LLC
Chambersburg PA
CBHW051709090426
42736CB00013B/2620